Did

CHEL

A M

```
CW00687409
```

Compiled by Julia Skinner

With particular reference to the work of Robin Brooks

THE FRANCIS FRITH COLLECTION

www.francisfrith.com

Based on a book first published in the United Kingdom in 2004 by The Francis Frith Collection®

This edition published exclusively for Oakridge Books & Gifts in 2010 ISBN 978-1-84589-547-1
Oakridge, Greenstalls Park, Costello Hill, Ilchester, Somerset BA22 8LB. Tel: 08453 893293

Text and Design copyright The Francis Frith Collection®
Photographs copyright The Francis Frith Collection® except where indicated.

The Frith® photographs and the Frith® logo are reproduced under licence from
Heritage Photographic Resources Ltd, the owners of the Frith® archive and trademarks.
'The Francis Frith Collection', 'Francis Frith' and 'Frith' are registered trademarks of
Heritage Photographic Resources Ltd.

All rights reserved. No photograph in this publication may be sold to a third party other than in the original
form of this publication, or framed for sale to a third party. No parts of this publication may be reproduced,
stored in a retrieval system, or transmitted, in any form, or by any means, electronic, mechanical, photocopying,
recording or otherwise, without the prior permission of the publishers and copyright holder.

British Library Cataloguing in Publication Data

Did You Know? Cheltenham - A Miscellany
Compiled by Julia Skinner
With particular reference to the work of Robin Brooks

The Francis Frith Collection
Frith's Barn, Teffont,
Salisbury, Wiltshire SP3 5QP
Tel: +44 (0) 1722 716 376
Email: info@francisfrith.co.uk
www.francisfrith.com

Printed and bound in England

Front Cover: **CHELTENHAM, CHELTENHAM COLLEGE PLAYING FIELDS 1907** 59038p

The colour-tinting is for illustrative purposes only, and is not intended to be historically accurate

AS WITH ANY HISTORICAL DATABASE, THE FRANCIS FRITH ARCHIVE IS CONSTANTLY BEING
CORRECTED AND IMPROVED, AND THE PUBLISHERS WOULD WELCOME INFORMATION ON
OMISSIONS OR INACCURACIES

CONTENTS

INTRODUCTION

Three centuries ago, Cheltenham was just a stone village on the edge of the Cotswolds. Its fortunes changed in 1715 when a health-giving mineral spring in the area was discovered, fashionable society arrived to take the waters and the spa town of Cheltenham was on the map. A pump room was constructed in 1738, and towards the end of the 18th century King George III gave the growing town the royal seal of approval by bringing his family to take the waters.

The handsome Promenade of the town was designed for the convenience of pedestrians: here the pavements are much wider than the roads, allowing the genteel residents and visitors to the spa to walk in safety away from the traffic, which was contained in narrow carriageways. It was for the building of the Promenade and the surrounding crescents and terraces that many of the quarries were opened in the neighbouring hills.

Cheltenham soon became a popular retirement home for military officers and colonial administrators who occupied elegant residences in its spreading Regency terraces, whilst others lived in purpose-built villas elsewhere in the developing town. However, not every visitor was impressed by the elegance of Cheltenham Spa. The radical writer and traveller William Cobbett (1763-1835) described Cheltenham as a 'nasty ill-looking place', full of 'East India plunderers, West Indian floggers, English tax-gorgers, … gluttons, drunkards and debauchers of all descriptions, female as well as male'. It is a safe guess that he did not enjoy his stay in the town!

Modern-day Cheltenham adorns the borderland between the western escarpment of the Cotswolds and the broad plain of the Vale of Gloucester like some architectural jewel; it remains a perfect Regency health spa, almost untouched at its heart by the unkind developments that ruined so many British towns during the 20th century.

CHELTENHAM, HIGH STREET 1901 47266

**CHELTENHAM, HIGH STREET
1906** 54320

GLOUCESTERSHIRE DIALECT WORDS AND PHRASES

'Adry' – thirsty.

'Airsens' – haws, the berries of the hawthorn tree.

'Artishrew' – the harvest mouse.

'Asker' – a newt.

'Badger' – a dealer in commodities in olden times, ie a butter dealer was known as a 'butter badger'.

'Candlemas bells' – snowdrops. (Candlemas Day is February 2nd.)

'Chubby' – the hedge-sparrow.

'Dabbly' – wet, rainy.

'Emmet' – an ant.

'Flummock' – a slovenly, untidy person.

'Ladycow' – ladybird.

'Maggot' – a magpie.

'Mugglement' – a state of muddle and confusion.

'Nettlesome' – quarrelsome.

'Watty-handed' – left-handed.

CHELTENHAM, PROMENADE 1923 73481

HAUNTED CHELTENHAM

A famous ghost story from the town is linked with a large house in Pittville Circus Road formerly known as Garden Reach, but now named St Anne's. The house was built in the 1860s by Henry Swithoe, but in 1882 it became the home of Captain Despard and his family. Soon after the family took up residence, one of the children saw a mysterious ghostly figure of a lady dressed in black. The apparition was then seen in the house by 17 other people between 1884 to 1886 before the visitations became less frequent, with the figure gradually appearing fainter and harder to see. The apparition seemed to roam through the house along a specific route, gliding down the stairs and into the main living room of the house, where it lingered for a moment before moving along a corridor to a door into the garden, where it suddenly vanished. At the time of the hauntings it was believed that the restless spirit was that of Henry Swinhoe's second wife, Imogen, whose unhappy marriage had driven her to drink. An exorcism was carried out in the early 1900s and the figure was not seen for some time, but in 1970 and 1985 there were again reports of a spectral woman being seen in the area around the house.

Many theatres around the country are said have a resident ghost, and Cheltenham's is no exception. The Everyman Theatre is said to be haunted by a mysterious figure that has been glimpsed in the upper circle of the auditorium, and a number of people have reported hearing the unexplained sound of music, usually by the main doors to the auditorium from the foyer. Amongst Cheltenham's haunted pubs are the Suffolk Arms where something eerie is said to lurk in the cellar and manifests itself in strange tapping noises when staff go down there.

Prestbury, on the outskirts of Cheltenham, also has its share of restless spirits. Among the phantom inhabitants that roam the area is the hooded figure of the Black Abbot, which glides across the churchyard before disappearing through a wall in the High Street…

CHELTENHAM, ST GREGORY'S CATHOLIC CHURCH c1955 C75080

9

Did You Know?

CHELTENHAM

A MISCELLANY

CHELTENHAM, PROMENADE 1931 83807

CHELTENHAM MISCELLANY

The first recorded mention of Cheltenham is in AD 803, in the seventh year of the reign of King Genwulf of Mercia. At the synod of Cloveshore in that year Denebreht, Bishop of Worcester and Wulfhard, Bishop of Hereford both claimed the right to rents paid by a church house that according to tradition stood in the quarter of Cheltenham now called Cambray. Denebreht declared that he had received these payments for 30 years past, which tells us that the religious foundation had been there since at least AD 773.

When the Iron Age promontory fort on Leckhampton Hill was excavated in 1969, an impressive construction was revealed. Double outer walls of limestone blocks laced with timbers were protected by a deep ditch and topped by a wooden palisade. The entrance was of a complex design and within the walled area fragments of pots were discovered, all of which hints that the people who lived there were members of a well ordered, sophisticated society.

In 1912 Cheltenham corporation held a competition for designs for municipal offices up to a budget of £10,000. A site was set aside in Imperial Gardens and a first prize of £100 was offered. All entries cost more than £10,000, so were all rejected. The corporation bought 5 private houses in a Promenade terrace then called Harward Buildings. The £5,500 price tag, plus the estimated £3,300 for conversion into Municipal Offices, was paid for by a loan from the Local Government Board. The corporation moved to its new residence in 1915 and has remained there ever since.

Brass studs are set into a pathway from the High Street to St Mary's churchyard. They were used as measure marks for tradesmen selling goods by the yard in the town's market. In 1226, Henry III granted the town a charter for a market, to be held each week on Thursday - and Thursday is still market day.

In 1578 Richard Pate founded Cheltenham Grammar School. Born in 1516, Pate was a lawyer, making his fortune as a government official. He became MP and Recorder for Gloucester and is buried in its cathedral. The original school was a two-storey building, standing in the High Street between Bennington and Henrietta Streets. It was one of the town's few stone buildings, used for three hundred years until it was replaced by a new school, built on the same site in 1889. In the 1960s the school moved to a new building, demolished in 1996.

In the early 17th century, a survey of Cheltenham was made by John Norden for the Crown landlord. It mentions two market houses, the Booth Hall where public business was conducted, and Market House, situated in the High Street opposite the Plough Inn, which stood more or less where the entrance to the Regent Arcade is found today. At about where the fountain outside Boots is now stood the town's High Cross. Close by was a lock-up where those who imbibed too freely of the locally made ale were put to recover.

When the town featured in the Manor Act of 1625 it was descriptively named Cheltenham Street, for that's what it was, a linear development of mostly half-timbered houses, punctuated by the occasional stone building, with alleys leading to open ground behind them. It is in the Manor Act that the spelling 'Cheltenham' first appears. Prior to that it had been variously Chinteneha, Chiltham, Chilteham, Chintenham, Chiltehe and Cheltham.

CHELTENHAM, HIGH STREET 1906 54319

**CHELTENHAM
THE COLLEGE PLAYING FIELDS 1907** 59038

In St Mary's parish church is an epitaph to Henry Skillicorne, the Manx sea captain who developed Cheltenham's first spa. It tells the story of how Skillicorne discovered the spring that resulted in Cheltenham's rise to fame and fashionable fortune in the 18th century. 'He was an excellent sea man of tryed courage', reads the epitaph, 'and could do business in seven tongues. He was so temperate as never to have been once intoxicated. Religious without hypocrisy, grave without austerity, of a cheerful conversation without levity, a kind husband and tender father'.

The Queen's Hotel was inspired by The Temple of Jupiter in Rome. It was built by Robert and Charles Jearrad, brothers and architects who moved the Imperial Spa down the Prom and reassembled it on the corner of St George's Road to make way for their grand design. The hotel opened on 21 July 1838, boasted over 70 bedrooms, and cost £47,000.

The pigeon is Cheltenham's symbol, seen on its coat of arms, as well as on signposts around the town centre. According to local legend, a Quaker, William Mason, bought a parcel of land at Bayshill in 1715. Strolling round his acquisition, he saw pigeons pecking at salt deposits at the edge of a spring. Mason realised that the growing popularity of drinking waters for health purposes meant that his natural resource could make money. He developed the spa in a small way, gradually adding facilities to cater for his patrons' needs, and advertising the virtues of his spring's purging powers.

The first recorded coach service from Cheltenham to London in 1738 completed the journey 'if God permitted in the short space of three days'. By 1770 a non-stop coach drawn by six horses ran the distance in 26 hours, an improvement, but still a daunting ordeal for passengers.

CHELTENHAM, NEPTUNE FOUNTAIN 1912 65100

The Ladies' College rose to prominence under the headship of Dorothea Beale, a radical thinker who believed that girls should have the same educational opportunities as boys. She also insisted that women should take plenty of physical exercise and perhaps by way of demonstrating the point, learned to ride a bicycle at the age of 67 in 1898. Despite having hands stricken with gout, the Principal of England's foremost school for girls was seen wobbling about the environs of Montpellier accompanied by a white-gloved page boy who was engaged to give her a push up the hills.

In the mid-18th century Cheltenham was still no more than a one-street market town, but its spa waters attracted the rich and famous. Visiting celebrities included George Frideric Handel, Samuel Johnson, the poet William Shenstone and a glamorous array of aristocrats. On 11 August 1743, for example, the town was temporary home to a duke and duchess, one earl, five lords and ladies, two knights, a judge, and two priors, plus a gaggle of lesser gentry.

Examples of Cheltenham's first electric street lamps can be seen today in the parish churchyard, Crescent Place, Trafalgar Street and elsewhere. The Onion and Dragon lamp standards were designed by borough engineer Joseph Hall. Made of cast iron by McDowall, Stevens & Company, they cost £9 15s 0d (£9.75) apiece. The town's first electricity generating station opened in Arle Road in 1891. Plans to use electricity to light the streets were made in 1896 and on 6 February 1897 the Mayoress turned on 29 electric arc lamps along the High Street, Ambrose Street and Clarence Street, replacing 75 gas lamps.

According to legend, the Devil's Chimney on Leckhampton Hill rises straight from the bowels of Hell (see photograph 47256 pages 18-19). Another story tells that it was carved by Oliver Cromwell's cannon. In 1897 the geologist S S Buckman said the formation was the result of 'natural differential erosion', but it is a remnant of the days when limestone was worked, though why quarrymen created this landmark is open to speculation.

British Medical Association.
THE LADIES' COLLEGE

CHELTENHAM, LADIES COLLEGE 1901 47275

CHELTENHAM, DEVIL'S CHIMNEY 1901 47256

CHELTENHAM, TOWN HALL 1923 73488

In 1786 the Town and Paving Commissioners met to regulate sanitation. A report said: 'In the borough was situate 6,541 houses, out of which number only 736 were belonging to the Cheltenham Sewers Company, so that upwards of 5,000 houses had no legal outlet and might be compelled to stop up their drains and have resort to the contaminating practice of cesspools. These private sewers mostly emptied themselves in the Chelt, and so polluted the stream (once so celebrated for its purity as to yield fish in quantity) that effluvia arising from it rendered it a public nuisance.'

Cheltenham's development as a spa resort received a meteoric boost when on 12 July 1788, on the advice of his doctors, George III arrived with his family and entourage. The royal party spent just over a month in the town, which made it the pre-eminent fashionable resort in the land. Accompanying George was his wife Queen Charlotte, who was a German princess from Mecklenburg-Strelitz. She was said to be so unattractive in appearance that when George met her for the first time he turned pale. Love conquered all though, and the devoted couple had 15 children in 21 years.

George III suffered from porphyria, a rare genetic disorder that in a short space of time resulted in his being labelled a lunatic and restrained in a strait-jacket. The early signs of this rapidly-progressing disease were physical, a rash, nausea, cramps and difficulty in breathing, all of which his doctors blamed on his majesty failing to change wet stockings. Mood swings became increasingly pronounced and George on occasion blabbered away for hours, unable to stop talking gibberish. He burst into tears for no reason, suffered convulsions, fell into a coma and on recovering consciousness tried to kill his son.

Harold Webb, owner of the town's largest brickworks, founded the Cotswold Hills Club in 1902. The success of the venture was made possible by the tram service to the hill, which opened the year before giving easy and cheap access to the course for all.

In July 1831 Nicolo Paganini arrived to perform two concerts during race week. Mr De Ville, manager of the Assembly Rooms, booked Paganini for a third show. As the auditorium filled with fans who'd paid twice the normal price, Nicolo argued that he should receive two-thirds of the door takings. 200 guineas was De Ville's best offer. Paganini stormed out of the hall and back to the Plough Hotel. Then the audience stormed out of the hall and into the Plough. So threatening was the music-loving mob that Nicolo was forced to return with his Stradivarius and perform.

CHELTENHAM, PROMENADE 1907 59032

The proprietor of the weekly 'Cheltenham Looker-on' newspaper wrote: 'The Almighty in his earliest laws expressed the need for providing bodily sustenance for the poor, but there was no positive Commandment for supplying their mental wants'.

In the 50 years following the visit of George III, Cheltenham grew at a remarkable pace. The spa was at its most brilliant and new wells were opened to meet growing demand. After the original Royal Old Well came the Montpellier Spa, Sherborne Well, Cambray Spa, Alstone Spa and Pittville. Hundreds of new houses were built. The population, 3000 in 1801, grew to 20,000 by 1826, accompanied by a frenzy of building speculation. This provided one of the major employment opportunities, for between 1815 and 1840 the great estates of Lansdown, Bayshill, Montpellier and Pittville appeared.

The Promenade was laid out in 1818, and land along its length was sold for development. The first shop, a draper's called Clark and Debenham, opened in 1823. Clark and Debenham had another store near Cavendish Square in London and the Cheltenham outlet, in business on the same site today, became known as Cavendish House. Also in 1823 a grand building appeared opposite. It was home to a painter named Millet. When he left, the house became the Imperial Hotel, then in 1856 the Imperial Club for 'resident noblemen and gentlemen'. The building now houses the Waterstone's bookshop.

Prestbury Park racecourse was converted into a 100-bed hospital in World War I and received its first influx of wounded soldiers on 28 October 1914. A fully equipped operating theatre was installed complete with electric lighting. Belgian, British, Canadian and French casualties from the trenches were ferried by ship to Southampton, then on to Cheltenham aboard special trains.

Christ Church is Cheltenham's finest example of 19th-century Gothic architecture. Built between 1837-1840, the land was donated by Pearson Thompson who developed the Montpellier estate. It was originally intended to build Christ Church 120 yards to the east of its eventual location, because parishioners at St James's said the new church was too close to their own. The design was by local architect brothers Robert and Charles Jearrad. The cost of the building was £18,111, the most expensive church in town up to that time.

In 1847, seven students began their teacher training course in a rented house. The foundation stone of St Paul's College was laid on 1 April 1849 by the Earl of Shaftesbury. It occupied a five-acre site in Swindon Road, donated by Miss Jane Cook. The architect was Samuel Whitfield Daukes, also responsible for Lansdown railway station, St Peter's church and Cirencester Agricultural College. He developed The Park area of Cheltenham, where he lived in a wonderful gothic fantasy of a house named Tudor Lodge (now recalled in Tudor Lodge Road), wickedly demolished in the mid-1960s.

Cheltenham Winter Gardens was constructed in 1879 to a design by J T Darby. The intention was to provide 'A large concert room …calculated to afford recreation and amusement to the upper classes'. In fact the place was largely unsuitable for anything much. It had dreadful acoustics. Rain on the roof could drown out concert performers. Various proprietors couldn't make it pay. In 1895 the town council bought the building. It became a roller-skating rink, then a cinema. Then the Town Hall was built in 1904 - next door. It was decided to demolish the Winter Gardens in September 1940.

Cheltenham had a full-time fire brigade in 1813, run by an insurance company, but providing a service only to private subscribers. Then the Town Commissioners paid the insurance company for fire-brigade services as and when required. But fire-fighting arrangements remained inadequate throughout the 19th century. Without acts of charity, there would hardly have been any provision at all. A public-spirited local lady, Mrs Theobalds bought the town a couple of fire engines, but it wasn't until the early 20th century that the town had its first fire station, opened in St James's Square at a cost of £993.

CHELTENHAM, CHRIST CHURCH 1906 54339

CHELTENHAM, PITTVILLE GARDENS
1923 73511

When the foundation stone of Cheltenham's public library in Clarence Street, (then Manchester Street) was laid on 21 June 1887, people massed to watch the ceremony. The town's first public library had opened in temporary premises in Liverpool Place five years before. The notion of a free public lending library had been mooted in 1855, but local ratepayers thought it an unnecessary financial burden.

Cheltenham may have been the first place in Britain to have letter-boxes on its streets. John Goding's history, published in 1863, relates: '1854, August. First pillar letter boxes erected at Cheltenham'. London didn't have letter-boxes until April 1855. These early letter-boxes stood about four feet high and were made of cast iron at Butt's foundry in Gloucester. To send a letter before pillar-boxes you took it to the post office and hoped! Cheltenham's first post office opened in 1800 at 127, High Street. Deliveries were sometimes only once a week .

Cheltenham's oldest surviving letter-boxes are hexagonal and known as Penfold boxes (named after their designer), which became post office standard issue in 1866. They were cast at a foundry in Dudley and examples can be seen in College Lawn, Montpellier Drive, Bayshill Road, Pittville Circus Road, Lansdown Crescent, Duoro Road and at the junction of Evesham Road with Cleevelands Drive. There's another at the museum in Clarence Street, which was in use until about 20 years ago and stood near the Queen's Road/ Gloucester Road roundabout.

Herbert Henry Martyn established his company of art craftsmen in premises on the corner of College Road and the High Street in 1888. Later the company moved to a 12.5-acre site, now Lansdown Industrial Estate. This remarkable company built aeroplanes (one of which holds a speed record to this day), motor cars (including parts of Henry Seagrave's world speed record winning car 'Golden Arrow') and fitted out over 100 of the world's greatest ocean liners. It made metalwork for important buildings in London, including the Cenotaph. Martyn's also produced wood and plasterwork for many royal palaces round the world.

Arthur Inglis, who was a pupil at Cheltenham College, holds a unique position in the history of tank warfare. Born on 4th July 1884, Inglis joined the Glosters at the outbreak of World War I.
He was the first man in history to lead tanks into action and he did so on foot, the traditional way for cavalry commanding officers, in 1916 at the battle of Flers Courcelles in the Somme sector. Remarkably, Inglis survived this ordeal, but was injured in 1918 and died a year later from his wounds. Major Arthur Inglis is buried in Prestbury churchyard.

In 1885 Lansdown residents wanted an ornamental lamp standard. Then residents decided their lamp would be erected to the memory of General Gordon, killed at Khartoum later that year. A public appeal for funds was made.... and £20 trickled in. As the chosen light cost £200 the organisers had to make up the difference. Then there was the question of who would pay for illumination. The granite base was late arriving. The ironwork had to be modified. Further expense was incurred when the lamp was converted to electricity in 1900. A plaque commemorating General Gordon was not added until 1933.

CHELTENHAM, SANDFORD PARK, ENTRANCE 1931 83810

CHELTENHAM, FASHION 1931 83807X

Cheltenham's slum clearance programme in the 1930s swept away dilapidated areas at the town's west end. Swindon Place was a terrace of 28 back-to-backs built in the 1820s to house the town's labouring and unemployed classes. Three earth closet privies were shared, which did nothing for the health of residents. Each house had a flagstone-floored living room 14 feet square in which was a hearth and oven. Upstairs were two small bedrooms. None of the houses had a bathroom, a few had mains water, most shared a communal pump. The rent in 1930 was 6/6d (33p) a week.

The Promenade was the town's showpiece. For the fashion-conscious it was the place to see and be seen. There's a story that in the 1920s, when the Prom was considered strictly a no-go area for the 'hoi polloi', the prosperous owner of Banks' (a well-known retailer) raised his hat to a probably impecunious minor-titled lady customer on his way to work. In the following morning's post he received a letter of sharp rebuke, making it quite clear that she did not wish to be acknowledged in public - and certainly not in the Promenade - by a mere tradesman.

CHELTENHAM, QUEEN'S HOTEL 1923 73492

On 22 August 1901 Cheltenham's inaugural tram service ran from Lansdown Castle to Cleeve Hill. 'At last the trams are here!' wrote the 'Gloucestershire Graphic'. Two days before, a tramcar descending Cleeve Hill on a trial run went out of control and overturned at Southam curve, killing two workmen. Once installed, however, the tramcars proved popular, and in their first week of operation carried 40,000 fare-paying passengers. Cheltenham's line was three feet six inches in gauge, rather than the four feet, eight-and-a-half inches found elsewhere. The tram era closed in Cheltenham at the end of 1930.

The former Coliseum cinema (now Springboks snooker club) showed its first film in 1931, but opened as Gilsmith's Hippodrome, a variety theatre, on 22 September 1913. Jack Judge is said to have written 'It's a long way to Tipperary' in the number one dressing room and first performed the song on the Albion Street theatre's stage. 'Bonnie and Clyde' was the last film seen at the Coliseum on 22 June 1974.

The architect of the former Gaumont Palace, which showed its first picture in 1933, was W E Trent. His cousin N A Trent designed the low relief figures that can still be seen on the façade. On 16 December 1962 the Gaumont became the Odeon, where on 1 November 1963 the Beatles played the opening date of their UK tour. Many other live acts appeared in the 1950s and '60s. The Rolling Stones topped the bill a number of times. Packed audiences came to see Cheltonian and founder member Brian Jones.

CHELTENHAM, LONDON ROAD 1906 54321

Government Communications Headquarters (GCHQ) arrived in Cheltenham by chance in the early 1950s because its forerunner, the government Code and Cypher School based at Bletchley Park, needed more space. The Benhall site, built in World War II as the administrative centre for the American Forces of Supply, was vacant. Oakley, another wartime site, was also looking for a new purpose, so out of expediency Bletchley Park moved to Cheltenham, where it remains to this day and is the town's major employer. In 2004 GCHQ moved to new premises at Benhall. The building is known locally as the Doughnut.

CHELTENHAM, THE STRAND, HIGH STREET 1931 83801

The 32 Greek-inspired armless women of Montpellier Walk, each with a decorative lintel resting on her head, are caryatids. They separate the shops that were built during the 1830s (see photograph C75714 opposite). Two were fashioned in terracotta by Charles Rossi (1762-1839), an English sculptor who lived in London and was responsible for many monuments in St Paul's cathedral. A Cheltenham chap named W G Brown was enrolled to copy 29 caryatids at his workshop in Tivoli Street. The remaining one was cast in concrete and added in 1970 when an extension was added to the building that is now a restaurant named Ask.

The Town Hall, designed by Gloucester architect Frederick Waller, was built in the first years of the 20th century to replace the Assembly Rooms. In an unsuccessful attempt to reverse the decline in popularity of Cheltenham as a health resort, the Central Spa was opened in the Town Hall in 1906. You can take the waters there to this day, but you'll have to help yourself. There are no maids to serve any more. To the rear of the Town Hall stood the Winter Gardens. One of the corner tower bases remains, behind the open air bar in Imperial Gardens.

CHELTENHAM, THE CENTRE 1937 87925

CHELTENHAM, A CARYATID IN MONTPELLIER 2004 C75714

Some six million tourists come to Cheltenham each year. For many the Promenade epitomises the town. It extends in a tree-lined, straight stretch for just over a quarter of a mile, bordered by broad pavements with fine shops on one side, buildings and grand gardens on the other. 'The Times' once eulogised it as 'The most beautiful thoroughfare in Britain'. In the early 19th century, the land now occupied by the Prom was a marshy bog, boasting nothing more than a few cottages. The widow of Spenser Percival lived in one after her husband, the Prime Minister, was assassinated.

Cheltenham's best-known item of street furniture stands in the Prom. Neptune's Fountain was designed by the borough surveyor Joseph Hall, who modelled it on Rome's Fontana di Trevi. Carved from Portland stone, the extravaganza first gushed on 30 October 1893. It commemorates nothing and is in memory of nobody, but was part of a general scheme to perk up the Prom. At one time a weeping willow grew within the ornamental fountain's stone balustrade, said to have been taken from the cutting of a tree that shaded Napoleon's final resting place on St Helena.

When Lloyds Bank bought the Montpellier Spa building for £14,000 in 1961, the place was in a sorry state. A survey revealed that the dome, 160 feet in diameter, and 60 feet high, had dropped three inches and was sagging on rotted roof beams. Two tons of copper and another two of lead were removed in the restoration, along with more tons of ornate plaster. When the former ballroom beneath the rotunda was stripped, the walls were found to be mirror-lined.

CHELTENHAM, THE NEPTUNE FOUNTAIN 1937 87921

Cheltenham Ladies' College occupies the land where the town's first mineral spring was discovered. The town's second public school, it was founded in 1854 in a house in Cambray. In 1873 the buildings seen here were constructed on the corner of St George's Road and Montpellier Street. The architect, John Middleton, was also responsible for a number of Cheltenham's churches, including St Stephen's and All Saints, Pittville. The precise location of the original spa is said to be covered by the college's Princess Hall, built on the site of the the Royal Wells Music Hall, later the Theatre Royal.

SPORTING CHELTENHAM

Cheltenham is famous for hosting the annual Cheltenham Cricket Festival, which is the oldest cricket festival in the world. As early as 1769 the 'Gloucester Journal' noted that Cheltenham was a cricket centre. The original county side, formed on 3rd November 1863, was the Cheltenham and County of Gloucestershire Club. The side played for the first time at Lord's against the MCC in 1868 – and won. It included three brothers, EM, GF and WG Grace – the latter being one of the most famous names in cricketing history. The team was renamed Gloucestershire County Cricket Club in 1871. The first 'cricket week' at the Cheltenham College ground (it wasn't called a festival until 1906) was organised in 1878 by James Lillywhite, the College coach, and cost £120 to stage.

Cheltenham Croquet Club is one of the largest croquet clubs in the country, as well as one of the three oldest – it was founded in 1869, in the same year as the croquet clubs in Brighton and Wimbledon. Cheltenham is also where the headquarters of the national Croquet Association is based.

At various times in its history Montpellier Gardens has hosted the town's croquet and archery clubs, while in the 19th century hot air balloons were launched and an early display of parachute jumping given.

Cheltenham's Lido is located in Sandford Park. This open-air swimming pool was built in May 1935, at a time when such facilities were appearing in many towns and cities. Today, however, lidos of this period are a rarity and Cheltenham is fortunate to have this architectural gem, which is well supported by local swimmers. It is one of the largest open air swimming pools in the country.

On the outskirts of Cheltenham at Prestbury is Cheltenham Racecourse, where National Hunt (jump racing) meetings are held from October to April. The course hosts the world-famous Cheltenham Festival in March, the highlight of which is the Cheltenham Gold Cup, one of the most prestigious events of National Hunt racing. The Cheltenham Gold Cup is an event for horses aged five years or older, run over a distance of 3 miles and 2½ furlongs (5,331 metres), with twenty-two fences.

Another sporting 'festival' in the town is the Cheltenham Rugby Festival; held in May, this is an event for rugby league nines.

CHELTENHAM, THE COLLEGE GROUND 1907 59039A

Did You Know?
CHELTENHAM
A MISCELLANY

CHELTENHAM, HIGH STREET
1901 47265

QUIZ QUESTIONS

Answers on page 50.

1. On the Promenade near the Cavendish House department store is a most unusual, and even controversial, piece of modern artwork – what does it depict?

2. In which Cheltenham shopping mall can you find a glass case displaying a model of a jet aeroplane, and why is it there?

3. Who was the Cheltenham-born composer (despite his foreign-sounding name) who wrote the famous 'Planet Suite'?

4. The statue of which polar explorer stands in the Promenade?

5. There is a statue in Prestbury Park to a famous Irish racehorse that won the Cheltenham Gold Cup three years in a row – what was the horse's name?

6. What is the oldest building in Cheltenham?

7. A much-loved feature of the Regent Arcade is the Wishing Clock. Which famous writer and artist designed it, and what does the clock do every half hour?

8. What is the nickname of Cheltenham Town Football Club?

9. On which Cheltenham housing estate are the roads named after poets?

10. Cheltenham's Latin motto is 'Salubritas et Eruditio'. What does this mean?

CHELTENHAM, UPPER PROMENADE 1901 47264

RECIPE

CHELTENHAM PUDDING

175g/6oz plain flour
1 teaspoonful baking powder
Half a teaspoonful grated nutmeg
A pinch of salt
175g/6oz shredded suet
75g/3oz sugar
75g/3oz fresh breadcrumbs
50g/2oz raisins
50g/2oz currants
Grated rind of half a lemon
2 eggs, beaten
150ml/ ¼ pint milk

Pre-heat the oven to 190°C/375°F/Gas Mark 5.

Sift the flour, baking powder, nutmeg and salt together into a mixing bowl. Mix in the suet, sugar, breadcrumbs, dried fruit and lemon rind. Stir in the beaten eggs and milk. Beat the mixture well to make a stiff, smooth batter.

Pour the batter into a greased ovenproof dish and bake in the pre-heated oven for 1½ hours. When cooked, turn out and serve with either a sweet sauce, custard or cream.

RECIPE

APPLE COBBS

Apple Cobbs is the Gloucestershire name for Apple Dumplings, which can be made with either shortcrust or suetcrust pastry.

> 4 large cooking apples
> 50g/2oz soft brown sugar
> 25g/1oz butter
> Half a teaspoonful ground cinnamon
> Grated rind of 1 lemon
> 225g/8oz shortcrust or suetcrust pastry, as preferred
> Milk to glaze
> Caster sugar

Pre-heat the oven to 180°C/350°F/Gas Mark 4.

Peel and core the apples. Divide the pastry into four equal pieces. Roll each piece out into a square big enough to wrap around an apple. Place one apple in the centre of each square. Mix the sugar, lemon peel and cinnamon together and use the mixture to fill the cavity of each apple, and place a knob of butter on top of the mixture.

Dampen the edges of each piece of pastry with water, and fold up the corners to meet at the top like a parcel, and enclose each apple. Pinch the pastry edges well together to seal.

Place the dumplings – join downwards – in a greased ovenproof dish and brush with milk to glaze. Bake in the pre-heated oven for about half an hour – test by sticking a skewer into the dumpling to make sure the apple is soft. Sprinkle with caster sugar, and serve with custard or cream.

QUIZ ANSWERS

1. The striking bronze statue on the Promenade depicts a hare and a minotaur. It is the work of artist Sophie Ryder and was cast by Pangolin Editions of Chalford, Stroud.

2. The Regent Arcade. Frank Whittle, 'the father of jet propulsion', assembled Britain's first jet engine in 1940/41 in the old Regents Motors Garage, which formerly stood on the site of the Regent Arcade.

**CHELTENHAM
"THE MINOTAUR & THE HARE"
SCULPTURE 2004** C75711

3. Gustav Holst, born in Cheltenham in 1874. His birthplace in Clarence Road is now the Holst Birthplace Museum, which not only provides a home for many of the musician's possessions, including his piano, but also presents authentic room sets of what a home looked and felt like in 19th-century Cheltenham.

4. Dr Edward Wilson, polar explorer and scientist, who was born in Cheltenham in 1872. He perished in the Antarctic with Captain Scott whilst making the homeward journey from the South Pole in 1912.

5. Arkle. This very popular horse won the Cheltenham Gold Cup in 1964, 1965 and 1966.

6. St Mary's Parish Church, in the town centre, started in the 12th century and completed in the 14th century. It is the town's only ancient building and an architectural gem.

7. The Wishing Clock was designed by Kit Williams, whose book 'Masquerade' in the 1970s sparked off a national treasure hunt for a bejewelled golden hare. Amongst many other delights, below the Wishing Clock hangs a large wooden fish that blows bubbles every half hour, to the accompaniment of tunes including 'I'm Forever Blowing Bubbles'. If you can catch one of the bubbles you can make a wish – hence the name of the clock.

8. The Robins, after the bright red colour of their home strip.

9. St Marks. This 115-acre site was bought by the corporation in 1919 to be developed as a housing estate, one of the first council house developments in the country. About 600 houses were built, lining roads named after Milton, Tennyson, Shelley, Kipling and other poets. These modest red brick semis capture the values of the Arts and Crafts Movement in their detailing and visual interest, and the St Marks estate is now a conservation area.

10. Cheltenham's Latin motto of 'Salubritas et Eruditio' means 'Health and Education'.

Did You Know?
CHELTENHAM
A MISCELLANY

CHELTENHAM, HIGH STREET 1937 87923

FRANCIS FRITH

PIONEER VICTORIAN PHOTOGRAPHER

Francis Frith, founder of the world-famous photographic archive, was a complex and multi-talented man. A devout Quaker and a highly successful Victorian businessman, he was philosophical by nature and pioneering in outlook. By 1855 he had already established a wholesale grocery business in Liverpool, and sold it for the astonishing sum of £200,000, which is the equivalent today of over £15,000,000. Now in his thirties, and captivated by the new science of photography, Frith set out on a series of pioneering journeys up the Nile and to the Near East.

INTRIGUE AND EXPLORATION

He was the first photographer to venture beyond the sixth cataract of the Nile. Africa was still the mysterious 'Dark Continent', and Stanley and Livingstone's historic meeting was a decade into the future. The conditions for picture taking confound belief. He laboured for hours in his wicker dark-room in the sweltering heat of the desert, while the volatile chemicals fizzed dangerously in their trays. Back in London he exhibited his photographs and was 'rapturously cheered' by members of the Royal Society. His reputation as a photographer was made overnight.

VENTURE OF A LIFE-TIME

By the 1870s the railways had threaded their way across the country, and Bank Holidays and half-day Saturdays had been made obligatory by Act of Parliament. All of a sudden the working man and his family were able to enjoy days out, take holidays, and see a little more of the world.

With typical business acumen, Francis Frith foresaw that these new tourists would enjoy having souvenirs to commemorate their days out. For the next thirty years he travelled the country by train and by pony and trap, producing fine photographs of seaside resorts and beauty spots that were keenly bought by millions of Victorians. These prints were painstakingly pasted into family albums and pored over during the dark nights of winter, rekindling precious memories of summer excursions. Frith's studio was soon supplying retail shops all over the country, and by 1890 F Frith & Co had become the greatest specialist photographic publishing company in the world, with over 2,000 sales outlets, and pioneered the picture postcard.

FRANCIS FRITH'S LEGACY

Francis Frith had died in 1898 at his villa in Cannes, his great project still growing. By 1970 the archive he created contained over a third of a million pictures showing 7,000 British towns and villages.

Frith's legacy to us today is of immense significance and value, for the magnificent archive of evocative photographs he created provides a unique record of change in the cities, towns and villages throughout Britain over a century and more. Frith and his fellow studio photographers revisited locations many times down the years to update their views, compiling for us an enthralling and colourful pageant of British life and character.

We are fortunate that Frith was dedicated to recording the minutiae of everyday life. For it is this sheer wealth of visual data, the painstaking chronicle of changes in dress, transport, street layouts, buildings, housing and landscape that captivates us so much today, offering us a powerful link with the past and with the lives of our ancestors.

Computers have now made it possible for Frith's many thousands of images to be accessed almost instantly. The archive offers every one of us an opportunity to examine the places where we and our families have lived and worked down the years. Its images, depicting our shared past, are now bringing pleasure and enlightenment to millions around the world a century and more after his death.

For further information visit: www.francisfrith.com

INTERIOR DECORATION

Frith's photographs can be seen framed and as giant wall murals in thousands of pubs, restaurants, hotels, banks, retail stores and other public buildings throughout Britain. These provide interesting and attractive décor, generating strong local interest and acting as a powerful reminder of gentler days in our increasingly busy and frenetic world.

FRITH PRODUCTS

All Frith photographs are available as prints and posters in a variety of different sizes and styles. In the UK we also offer a range of other gift and stationery products illustrated with Frith photographs, although many of these are not available for delivery outside the UK – see our web site for more information on the products available for delivery in your country.

THE INTERNET

Over 100,000 photographs of Britain can be viewed and purchased on the Frith web site. The web site also includes memories and reminiscences contributed by our customers, who have personal knowledge of localities and of the people and properties depicted in Frith photographs. If you wish to learn more about a specific town or village you may find these reminiscences fascinating to browse. Why not add your own comments if you think they would be of interest to others? See **www.francisfrith.com**

PLEASE HELP US BRING FRITH'S PHOTOGRAPHS TO LIFE

Our authors do their best to recount the history of the places they write about. They give insights into how particular towns and villages developed, they describe the architecture of streets and buildings, and they discuss the lives of famous people who lived there. But however knowledgeable our authors are, the story they tell is necessarily incomplete.

Frith's photographs are so much more than plain historical documents. They are living proofs of the flow of human life down the generations. They show real people at real moments in history; and each of those people is the son or daughter of someone, the brother or sister, aunt or uncle, grandfather or grandmother of someone else. All of them lived, worked and played in the streets depicted in Frith's photographs.

We would be grateful if you would give us your insights into the places shown in our photographs: the streets and buildings, the shops, businesses and industries. Post your memories of life in those streets on the Frith website: what it was like growing up there, who ran the local shop and what shopping was like years ago; if your workplace is shown tell us about your working day and what the building is used for now. Read other visitors' memories and reconnect with your shared local history and heritage. With your help more and more Frith photographs can be brought to life, and vital memories preserved for posterity, and for the benefit of historians in the future.

Wherever possible, we will try to include some of your comments in future editions of our books. Moreover, if you spot errors in dates, titles or other facts, please let us know, because our archive records are not always completely accurate—they rely on 140 years of human endeavour and hand-compiled records. You can email us using the contact form on the website.

Thank you!

For further information, trade, or author enquiries
please contact us at the address below:

**The Francis Frith Collection, Frith's Barn, Teffont,
Salisbury, Wiltshire, England SP3 5QP.**
Tel: +44 (0)1722 716 376 Fax: +44 (0)1722 716 881
e-mail: sales@francisfrith.co.uk **www.francisfrith.com**